W9-CPE-001

THE LIBRARY OF WEAPONS OF MASS DESTRUCTION™

The
Atom Bomb
Creating and Exploding
the First Nuclear Weapon

TAMRA ORR

The Rosen Publishing Group, Inc., New York

RAP

Published in 2005 by The Rosen Publishing Group, Inc.
29 East 21st Street, New York, NY 10010

Copyright © 2005 by The Rosen Publishing Group, Inc.

First Edition

All rights reserved. No part of this book may be reproduced in any form without permission in writing from the publisher, except by a reviewer.

Library of Congress Cataloging-in-Publication Data

Orr, Tamra.
The atom bomb: creating and exploding the first nuclear weapon / by Tamra Orr.
    p. cm. — (The library of weapons of mass destruction)
Includes bibliographical references and index.
ISBN 1-4042-0292-7 (library binding)
1. Atomic bomb—United States—Juvenile literature. 2. Hiroshima-shi (Japan)—History—Bombardment, 1945. 3. Nagasaki-shi (Japan)—History—Bombardment, 1945
I. Title. II. Series.
UG1282.A8O77 2005
623.4'5119—dc22

                                                          2004011269

Manufactured in the United States of America

On the cover: The Fat Man bomb, which would explode over Nagasaki, Japan, is loaded onto a trailer cradle in August 1945.

[CONTENTS]

INTRODUCTION

E ver since a Greek man named Democritus
declared in 450 BC that everything in the world
is made of something called atoms, scientists have
been at work to figure out exactly what an atom is.
Lacking the ability to directly investigate the atom,
scientists could only form concepts of it. Did a
hard, impenetrable "mass" exist? Or was it a move-
ment that occurred within the elements? More
questions were asked: What is inside of it? How do
the different parts work? Can humans alter atoms?
What happens if we do?

This is the epicenter of the Trinity Test site. The first atom bomb was exploded here, at Alamogordo, New Mexico, on July 16, 1945. The heat of the explosion melted the sand below it into a glassy crust. In order to make this an accessible national historic site years later, the mildly radioactive layer was bulldozed and covered with soil.

Thousands of years ago in ancient China and later in Egypt, inquisitive men called alchemists were driven by the curiosity of what happens if one attempts to alter the elements. They tried to change copper into gold and lead into silver. If they could just combine the correct ingredients, they believed, it would happen! At the turn of the twentieth century, another set of scientists called physicists followed the alchemists' example. They were hard at work investigating the most basic particle on earth—the atom.

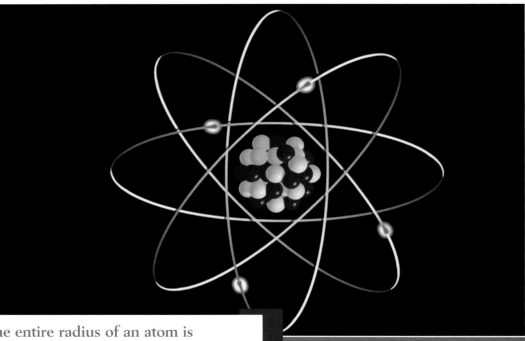

The entire radius of an atom is 0.00000001 centimeters. To give an idea of just how small that is, if 50 million atoms were lined up in a row, they would almost reach a centimeter. The nucleus contains protons and neutrons, while electrons move quickly around the nucleus in orbits. Besides these components, the atom is made up of empty space.

Their investigations of the atom led to discoveries that are still being built upon today. The discoveries also led in a direction that those early scientists had never considered. Understanding the atom's properties and then changing them would result in one of history's biggest moments: when the information went from a theory on paper to the atom bomb—a weapon of mass destruction. ■

Smoke billows from the explosion of the atom bomb over Hiroshima, Japan. The city was the primary target of the United States' attack mission. It contained the Japanese army headquarters that oversaw the defense for all of southern Japan. It was also a communication center, storage center, and a location where Japanese troops would gather.

ABOUT THE ATOM

Between 1896 and 1939, interest in atoms increased, and many different physicists were working hard to discover more about the atom and what could be done with the knowledge once they found it. In Great Britain, a physicist named J. J. Thomson (1856–1940) was experimenting with bending light rays by using strong magnets. In 1897, he discovered mysterious particles that he called corpuscles. After he announced his finding to others, these particles would finally be given the name electrons, tiny parts of atoms that carry a negative electric charge. This discovery started a

THE ATOM REVEALED: A TIMELINE

600 BC Thales taught that all matter is composed of water.

500 BC Heracleitus claimed that matter is made of fire.

450 BC Empedocles believed that matter is made of fire, air, earth, and water.

450 BC Democritus said that matter is made of different kinds of atoms.

1630 Pierre Gassendi said that atoms are hooked together.

1802 John Dalton thought that atoms differ in size and weight.

1867 Lord Kelvin said that atoms have shape.

1897 J. J. Thomson stated that the atom is a positively charged sphere with internal electrons.

1903 Philipp Lenard proposed that atoms are pairs called dynamids.

1904 Hantaro Nagaoka proposed that atoms have a nucleus and electrons.

1913 Niels Bohr assigned each electron a specific orbit to follow.

1932 James Chadwick proposed the existence of neutrons.

worldwide fascination with finding out more. If there were negative elements, for example, did that mean there were positive ones also? Were they scattered throughout the atom or centered in the middle?

One of Thomson's best students was a scientist named Ernest Rutherford (1871–1937), who was originally from New Zealand. An extremely intelligent man, Rutherford had earned honors in fields ranging from foreign languages and literature to math and physics. Taking up Thomson's research, he focused on learning more about the properties of the atom. He discovered that it was mostly made up of empty space with a central core, or nucleus, that contained protons, elements with a positive charge. Fifteen years later, English physicist James Chadwick (1891–1974) added to that information by discovering that atoms also contain neutrons, particles with no electrical charge. Their function seemed to be just to add mass to the atom.

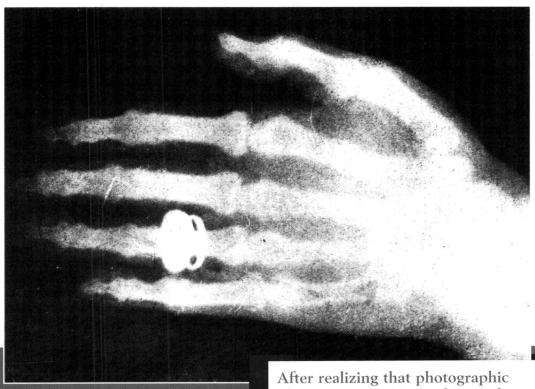

MEANWHILE, IN FRANCE . . .

At the end of the nineteenth century, while Rutherford and others were experimenting with which components make up the atom, other sci-

After realizing that photographic plates were sensitive to his newly discovered X-rays, Wilhelm Röntgen convinced his wife to participate in his experiments. She saw the resulting X-ray image as a sign of imminent death. Nevertheless, the image of her hand and her husband's discovery were soon displayed in newspapers all over Europe and the United States.

entists were intrigued with something equally mysterious. X-rays had already been discovered by a German physics professor named Wilhelm Conrad Röntgen (1945–1923) on November 8, 1895. Like Thomson, Röntgen had begun by working with bending light rays, but instead of paying attention to the stream of particles that had intrigued Thomson, he focused on the odd blue glow that appeared at the end of the highly evacuated light tube. What was it? It was a new kind of ray, and because he did not know what kind it was, Röntgen called it an X-ray. To his shock, he found that not only did it glow in the dark, but when the tube

was turned on, a piece of paper coated with specific chemicals that had been placed across the room also glowed. It was even more surprising when he took the piece of paper and put it in another room, and it still glowed! Apparently, the rays could pass right through the wall.

A physicist named Antoine-Henri Becquerel (1858–1902) was in Paris, trying to find out more about new elements that also seemed to be able to glow in the dark. Becquerel had heard about Röntgen's discovery and immediately wanted to learn more. Becquerel had been studying uranium and potassium that glowed, and he felt there might be a connection. Through a series of experiments, Becquerel eventually learned that the only substances that glowed, or fluoresced, contained uranium. Scientists Pierre and Marie Curie (1867–1934) , also in

The Curies, Marie and Pierre, are pictured here with a visitor *(far left)* at their laboratory in France. When Marie began to study the strange rays that came from uranium, she used an electrometer that her husband, Pierre, had invented years earlier. She was able to detect faint electric currents in the air, given off by the radioactive element, and reproduce her results. Her findings, which supported that of Antoine-Henri Becquerel, led to the Curies and Becquerel winning the Nobel Prize in Physics in 1903.

Paris, would come to the same conclusion. However, they took it to the next step to ask where uranium gets the energy to give off these rays. The Curies tested every metal they could find to see if any gave off rays. Besides uranium, the only other substance to give off rays was a dense, black mineral ore called pitchblende. Since pitchblende contains uranium, this made sense. What was puzzling was that pitchblende gave off stronger rays than uranium. To find out why, the Curies spent months breaking down tons of pitchblende into its separate elements. Finally, in 1898, they found an unknown element that gave off rays. They named it polonium in honor of their homeland, Poland. The couple coined the term "radioactive" for these special rays. Six months later, the Curies discovered another unfamiliar and very powerful element. They called this one radium.

As a young boy in Rome, Enrico Fermi discovered physics when he happened upon two elementary physics textbooks at an outdoor market. Grieving the recent loss of his older brother at the time, he consumed himself with the books, supposedly not even realizing they were written in Latin and not Italian.

The Sciences Come Together

By the 1930s, physicists all over the world were studying the radioactivity that the Curies had described. Enrico Fermi (1901–1954), an Italian physicist working in Rome, began systematically bombarding the elements in the periodic table with neutrons, beginning with the lightest, in an effort to induce radiation. His first success came with the element fluorine, although the radiation emitted was minimal. He finally made his way to uranium, the heaviest element known at the time. Fermi found that the lighter elements tended to transform into even lighter ones when bombarded with neutrons by ejecting, for example, a proton. However, heavier elements seemed to be made even heavier, due to the stronger electrical barrier around the nucleus that would capture the bombarding neutron and cause it to release its binding energy, therefore making the element a heavier isotope—having the same atomic number but different atomic mass—of itself. Because he first had to slow the neutrons down, Fermi shot them through both water and the waxy substance paraffin. In October 1934, when he finally managed to bombard uranium with these particles, something happened that he did not expect: the neutrons changed the uranium into two new elements. Fermi did not know why or what they were. He had no idea that he had just created the world's first atomic fission—the splitting of the atom.

A German physicist named Otto Hahn (1879–1968) found the solution four years later in 1938. Hahn suspected he had figured out what Fermi's two new elements were, but his answer was so odd and unexpected that he hesitated telling anyone else about it. He believed that the two elements were created because the nucleus of the uranium had been split in two when the neutrons hit it. One of the products was a radioactive form of the much lighter element barium. The other was thought to be krypton, a gas, which would have escaped immediately. The only person he would approach with this hypothesis was his longtime coworker, Austrian physicist Lise Meitner (1878–1968). She agreed with Hahn, prompting him to share his findings with others. A German chemist named Ida Noddack (1896–1978) had presented the same theory sometime earlier. However, because she had not established any credentials yet, her theory was overlooked. Ultimately, it was Hahn who received credit for realizing that Fermi had indeed produced atomic fission.

The news of what Hahn had discovered spread quickly. Within days, Meitner's nephew Otto Frisch (1886–1982) shared the news with one of the biggest experts in quantum mechanics, Danish physicist Niels Bohr (1885–1962). When he heard about the discovery, Bohr, who had hypothesized about atomic fission, could not believe his team had missed it all that time. On January 26, 1939, at the Fifth Annual Washington Conference of Theoretical Physics, Bohr announced Hahn's

IT'S CLEAR
Nicholson's Gin
IT'S GOOD

LATEST PRICES

LATE NIGHT FINAL

Evening Standard

La Coquille

No. 35,990   LONDON, FRIDAY, SEPTEMBER 1, 1939   ONE PENNY

GERMANS INVADE AND BOMB POLAND BRITAIN MOBILISES

Warsaw, Cracow, Nine Other Towns Bombed: Danzig is "Annexed"

FRANCE DECLARES "STATE OF SIEGE"

GERMANY INVADED POLAND TO-DAY. COMPLETE MOBILISATION HAS BEEN ORDERED IN BRITAIN.

Orders in Council for the complete mobilisation of the Navy, Army and Air Force were signed by the King at a Privy Council to-day. The King also approved other Orders in Council dealing with the emergency.

Warsaw has been bombed. Other German aircraft raided Kursk, Gdynia, Thorn, Bialystock, Grodno, Dibivö and Bydgoszcz. A few hours later, Cracow, Katowice and Czenstowice were bombed.

THE EVENING STANDARD LEARNS THAT THE POLISH AMBASSADOR SAW LORD HALIFAX TO-DAY. HE INFORMED THE FOREIGN SECRETARY OF THE GERMAN ATTACK UPON POLAND, WHICH HE SAID CONSTITUTED A CASE OF DIRECT AGGRESSION AND HE INVOKED THE ANGLO-POLISH TREATY.

French aid has also been invoked.

The French Cabinet met for an hour and 35 minutes. They decided to call Parliament immediately, to order general mobilisation of Army, Navy and Air Force beginning to-morrow, and to proclaim a "state of siege."

The Germans attacked without having delivered any ultimatum.

Attack On Both Sides

They are striking at the "Corridor" both from the East and the West—from the East at the town of Dirklkown, on the East Prussian frontier, and from the West at Chojnice, about 60 miles from Danzig.

Dirklkown is about 80 miles north-west of Warsaw.

(Continued on PAGE FOUR)

Air Raid Warning System In Force

'BRITAIN WILL FULFIL HER OBLIGATIONS'

Parliament Meeting Tonight

THE BRITISH CABINET MET TO-DAY. THEY BROKE UP AFTER ONE HOUR AND FIFTY MINUTES.

BOTH HOUSES OF PARLIAMENT ARE MEETING AT SIX O'CLOCK TO-NIGHT. THE PRIME MINISTER IS MAKING A FULL STATEMENT IN THE COMMONS AND AFTERWARDS THE HOUSE IS BEING ASKED TO PASS EMERGENCY LEGISLATION AT ONCE AND TO VOTE CREDITS. LORD HALIFAX IS MAKING A STATEMENT IN THE LORDS.

MEMBERS OF PARLIAMENT WILL BE IN POSSESSION OF THE CORRESPONDENCE BETWEEN GREAT BRITAIN AND GERMANY WHICH WILL BE PUBLISHED IN A WHITE PAPER.

It was pointed out in official circles in London to-day that if the proclamation to the German people by Herr Hitler should mean, as it would seem to mean, that Germany has declared war on Poland, it can be stated on the highest authority that Great Britain and France are sedulously determined to fulfil to the utmost

(Continued on BACK PAGE)

The front page of London's *Evening Standard* newspaper on September 1, 1939. Fifty-six German divisions confronted thirty Polish divisions that were thinly lined up across the Polish front line. Hitler's superior aircraft arsenal quickly overtook the Polish defense. This was the beginning of the German blitzkreig that would devastate much of Europe. France and Great Britain declared war on Germany on September 3, 1939.

theory. A few days later, Frédéric Joliot-Curie, who had met and married Irene Curie, the daughter of Marie and Pierre, broadcast the news that he, too, had come to the same conclusion as Hahn. During the next year, scientists wrote more than 100 papers on the possibilities and properties of splitting the atom. Each report focused on a different aspect of what could be done with this amazing new energy source that had been discovered. Could it be used to power machinery? Fuel vehicles? Build the first rocket ship? It was not long before most researchers realized that within this concept of atomic fission was amazing power and energy like the world had never seen before.

Where did the energy come from in the bombardment of uranium atoms? According to Albert Einstein's equation for changing matter to energy, $E=mc^2$, a small amount of matter contains a large amount of energy. The mass of an atom is more than the individual masses of its protons and neutrons, a result of the atom's binding energy. When the uranium atom splits, this extra mass, or energy, is released as radiation.

Even as the headlines of these awesome discoveries ran in the newspapers, bigger, far more threatening ones replaced them. "Scientists Say Bit of Uranium Could Wreck New York" was easily eclipsed by "Britain Prepares for a Crisis as Hitler Threatens Poland." The year was 1939 and World War II (1939–1945) was looming ever closer on the horizon. Adolf Hitler's Nazi regime was advancing throughout Germany's neighboring countries after forcibly annexing Austria and Czechoslovakia. Now, it was clear that Europe was headed directly for war as city after city fell under German control. The United States hoped to stay neutral in this rising conflict. As the country was in the throes of the Great Depression, it wanted to stay focused on domestic affairs. Also, with the devastation and death toll of World War I (1914–1918) only two decades before, Americans were not ready for the prospect of another war.

Now, with the introduction of atomic fission's potential power, both political and military leaders on both sides of the imminent war would soon begin to look at this new discovery as much more than just new science. They began to see it as the edge needed to win this international battle. Before long, information about the tiniest particles in the world would be the answer to creating the biggest explosion in history. ■

2

FROM ATOMS
TO WEAPONS

The leap from splitting an atom to creating a bomb was neither quick nor easy. Every step made only created more unanswered questions and challenging obstacles. It was clear that energy was released when fission occurred, but how much energy? A single fission was clearly possible, but how about a chain of fissions? If one happens, can it trigger more? The topic of atomic energy appeared in countless magazines and newspapers, but none of them proposed any serious answers. As late as 1939, the possibility of an actual atom bomb (also called an atomic bomb) was still considered highly unlikely by most and impossible by others. Although the mere act of splitting the atom created energy, it was still beyond the scope of scientists to imagine it being powerful enough to create a bomb.

A LETTER FROM A FRIEND

In 1939, a Hungarian physicist named Leo Szilard (1898–1964), who now resided in the United States, was asking these same questions. He was becoming more and more frustrated that no one was finding any solutions. He was terribly concerned that if an atom bomb were possible, an idea he is said to have pondered as early as 1933, the Germans would figure out how to make one first. They had already stopped the newly occupied Czechoslovakia from selling the United States any more uranium ore. Szilard tried to convince Fermi that he should speed up his experiments in creating fission, but Fermi was cautious because he was still uncertain what potential was there and how it should and would be used.

Szilard was conducting his own experiments. He was trying to find out if each atomic fission would create "stray" neutrons, which could, in turn, trigger additional fissions. On March 3, 1939, he discovered that this was indeed possible. Because of Szilard's aggravation and worry that this new possibility was not being explored and that the Germans would discover it first, Szilard turned to a friend of his who happened to be one of the world's most famous scientists—Albert Einstein. Szilard knew that if he could enlist Einstein's support, a great deal of progress might be made toward developing the bomb.

Einstein was on vacation near the northern tip of Long Island, New York, when Szilard tried to contact him. In July 1939, Szilard and another physicist named Eugene Wigner (1902–1995) drove from Manhattan to Einstein's cabin. The three scientists, sitting on Einstein's porch, began discussing the recent research on uranium and

Albert Einstein and Leo Szilard are pictured here in a reenactment of the signing of their letter to Franklin D. Roosevelt that urged him to develop atomic energy research. The scientists warned the president that Germany was building a bomb with the new atomic fission technology.

the possibility of an atomic bomb. Szilard's request was an easy one: he wanted to know whether Einstein would write to his friend, the Belgian Queen Mother. He wanted him to warn her against selling any of her country's uranium ore to the Germans. Einstein agreed, only saying that he'd direct his letter to the Belgian ambassador instead, because he knew him better.

A few days later, however, the writing of this letter quickly became less important. Szilard got the unexpected opportunity to speak directly to Alexander Sachs, economist and unofficial advisor to President Franklin D. Roosevelt. Sachs told the scientist that if Einstein took the time to write to the president about the importance of further atomic study, he would personally deliver the letter to him. Szilard was excited! This could be the opportunity that he had hoped for all along.

Einstein agreed to write the letter although it was not an easy decision for him. He had been a lifelong pacifist, but like Szilard, he was terribly concerned that the Germans would get to this frightening technology first. After all, the process of atomic fission had been discovered in Germany by German scientists. Szilard sat down and wrote the first draft of the letter. He mailed it to Einstein and then the two men, along with physicist Edward Teller (1908–2003), met face-to-face once more on the cabin porch to discuss it.

Einstein did not care for Szilard's letter; he felt it was too long and awkward. He dictated a shorter version, mentioning the work of Szilard, Fermi, and Joliot (Irene Curie's husband and assistant to Marie and Pierre Curie). Szilard prepared both a long and short version of the letter. Although Einstein signed both of them, he at last preferred that the longer one be sent to the president.

IT'S ALL IN THE TIMING

Although the letter was dated August 2, it did not reach Roosevelt for more than two months. Sachs was trying to wait for just the right moment to approach Roosevelt with the plea to speed up work on a potential bomb. He wanted the president's full attention, and, unfortunately, Germany's invasion of Poland on September 1, 1939, was cause for delay. Because France and Great Britain had pledged support to

Poland in the event of German aggression, the two countries declared war on Germany two days later. With the war escalating, Roosevelt's mind was focused on the decision of whether or not the United States should enter into the conflict. He knew that it would mean something the country had never wanted—the beginning of World War II.

On October 11, 1939, the president finally read Einstein's letter. Although he still was not convinced that atomic energy was as important as Szilard believed it was, he agreed to appoint a Uranium Advisory Committee and allocated $6,000 for the materials and uranium Szilard needed to continue his experiments. This response was less than Szilard had hoped for, but neither he nor the president knew at the time that over the next six years, that figure would grow to more than $2 billion.

The next two years seemed to pass very slowly for the Uranium Advisory Committee. Under the

October 19, 1939

My dear Professor:

I want to thank you for your recent letter and the most interesting and important enclosure.

I found this data of such import that I have convened a Board consisting of the head of the Bureau of Standards and a chosen representative of the Army and Navy to thoroughly investigate the possibilities of your suggestion regarding the element of uranium.

I am glad to say that Dr. Sachs will cooperate and work with this Committee and I feel this is the most practical and effective method of dealing with the subject.

Please accept my sincere thanks.

Very sincerely yours,

Dr. Albert Einstein,
Old Grove Road,
Nassau Point,
Peconic, Long Island,
New York.

Here, Franklin D. Roosevelt responds to Albert Einstein in this letter dated October 19, 1939. "I found this data of such import that I have convened a Board . . . to thoroughly investigate the possibilities of your suggestion regarding the element uranium." The letter was Einstein's only contribution to the atom bomb project. Because of his German heritage, along with his pacifist political views, he was denied security clearance by the government.

leadership of Dr. Lyman Briggs, director of the Washington Bureau of Standards, sixteen projects were developed and $300,000 was spent working on the separation of the uranium atom and the logistics of how to create a chain reaction of fission. However, more money was needed, and more work had to be done.

In 1940, Hitler's armies were advancing with great power; Poland, Denmark, Hungary, Norway, Holland, Belgium, and France had already fallen. By September 1940, England was being bombed. In the summer of 1941, Germany struck out at Russia. On December 6, 1941, the U.S. government decided to step up work on atomic energy. The following morning, on December 7, the nation's attention would be focused on the Hawaiian naval base, Pearl Harbor. More than 180

A U.S. warship is on fire in Pearl Harbor, after the Japanese attack on December 7, 1941. The United States had embargoed war materials, including oil, and frozen Japanese assets in the United States as a reaction to Japanese imperial expansion throughout Asia. Japan was taking a gamble by attacking the United States, but with its diminishing supplies to support its expansion efforts, it felt it had very little to lose by attacking the United States.

Leslie Groves graduated from the University of Washington in 1914, then attended the Massachusetts Institute of Technology for two years where he studied engineering, before going to West Point, where he graduated fourth in his class. Before directing the Manhattan Project, Groves had overseen construction of the Pentagon. After World War II, he continued with atomic energy affairs until 1947, then retired from active duty.

Japanese aircraft and 60 ships attacked the base and killed almost 3,000 American military men and their families. Japan, in its aim to extend its empire throughout Asia, succeeded in disabling the U.S. Pacific fleet in this attack. However, its other goal—to discourage the United States from entering the war—was not reached. Almost immediately, the face of the war changed; now the country was far more interested in retaliation. Nine days after the attack, a meeting was held to discuss what could be done to speed up making the atom bomb a reality.

THE ARMY TAKES OVER

By early summer 1942, the atomic project had been turned over to the U.S. Army. Colonel James Marshall was given the charge of building and running the bomb's production facilities. His headquarters was located in New York City, and it was not long before the commission had a new nickname: the Manhattan Engineer District. Eventually, it would come to be known as the Manhattan Project.

Colonel Marshall then appointed career army colonel Leslie Groves to quicken the pace on this vital project. Groves was not happy about this position; he had planned on going to Europe to fight in the war. Staying in New York to oversee factory construction and monitor scientists was not as appealing to him. The appointment was not a choice, but to make the offer more appealing, he was promoted to brigadier general.

Groves was a good choice. He was not afraid to tackle some of the project's biggest problems and search for a solution. Since having enough uranium on hand was one of the challenges the Manhattan Project faced, one of the first actions Groves took was to buy a supply of uranium ore that had been sitting in a warehouse on Staten Island so that the scientists would have enough for their experiments. He also addressed one of the project's main dilemmas—finding enough of the right neutrons—even though it was beyond his capability.

Why was this difficult? When atoms have the same number of protons in their nuclei, they are given the same atomic number; they can, however, have a different number of neutrons in them. In uranium, most atoms have 92 protons and 146 neutrons (called U-238), but seven out of every thousand have 92 protons and 143 neutrons (known as U-235). Unfortunately, those seven are the ones that split the best and could work for a possible atomic chain reaction. Obviously, the U-235 was the one the scientists needed, but how could they possibly sort through uranium atoms to find them fast enough? It would be like being put into a room with thousands of bricks and having to find the seven that weighed three ounces less than the rest!

Different scientists had different theories. Some believed that these special atoms were best separated out magnetically, while others thought it was a thermal, or heat, process. Still others, including Fermi, believed that the solution was not in separating these atoms at all but pursuing another new element called plutonium. Groves, not knowing which theory was the best, decided to establish sites devoted to the development of all three. It was a gamble—and one that was costing millions of dollars.

TEST TIME

As 1942 ended, Fermi and other scientists were ready to build their first atomic reactor. They were relying on the fact that they would be able to prove that they could create a reactor that would fission and start a chain reaction of energy.

As usual, the scientists faced another set of problems. The neutrons being released during uranium fission moved too fast, and too many were lost to cause the chain reaction they were seeking. Fermi had once slowed down atomic elements by shooting them through water. He tried that again, but this time it did not work. The hydrogen in the water absorbed too many of the neutrons. Fermi thought that perhaps graphite, the material used in pencil leads, might be the solution. But his supply of graphite had a high content of boron, one of the best elements for absorbing neutrons. Fermi needed a huge amount of pure graphite—enough to fill a pencil for every human being on the planet. It was not easy to come by either. It took almost a year to gather, which slowed the project down.

As the graphite arrived, Fermi and others began to make a pile, or layers of pure graphite alternating with graphite imbedded with chunks of uranium. As the pile approached ceiling height, the group realized that the lab was not big enough. Soon, the Manhattan Project was moved to the University of Chicago, where there would be enough room for the entire project to be located at one site. This team was called the Metallurgical Laboratory, or Met Lab for short.

In Chicago, they found the perfect site for the first reactor test. It was an abandoned squash court under the west stands of Stagg Field at the University of Chicago stadium. Football had been banned at the college,

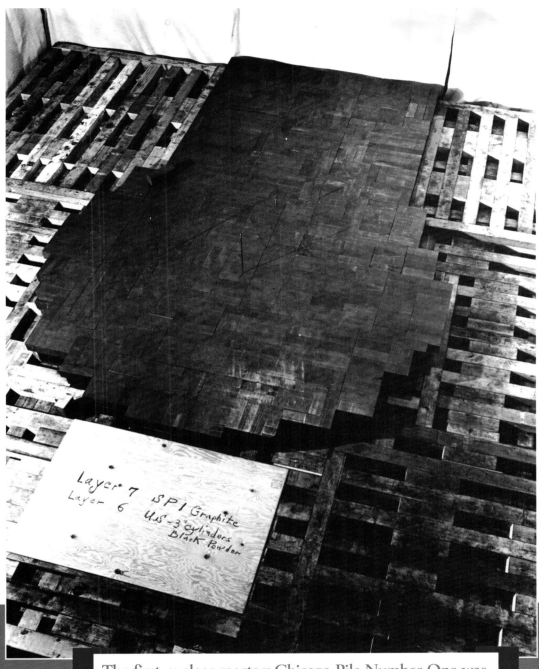

The first nuclear reactor: Chicago Pile Number One was built by Enrico Fermi's team. By the time the reactor was completed, it included 771,000 pounds (349,720 kg) of graphite, 80,590 pounds (36,551 kg) of uranium oxide, and 12,400 pounds (5,624 kg) of uranium metal. The pile cost 1 million dollars. The only visible action of the neutron and plutonium breeding stack was the movable pen as it gauged the nuclear chain reactions.

so the field was being used for miscellaneous activities. It proved to be the perfect testing site.

On the morning of December 2, 1942, a group of scientists, chemists, physicists, and others gathered around a 24-foot-wide (7.3 m) pile of sixty layers of graphite and uranium. It was enclosed within a large wooden frame that was 14 feet (4.3 m) tall. This was the defining moment when the future of the atomic bomb would be decided. If the chain reaction they hoped for did not occur, research on this bomb could easily come to a complete halt.

"We shall take measurements and verify that the pile will keep on acting as we have calculated."

Enrico Fermi

The three men who crawled on top of Chicago Pile Number One were laughingly referred to as the "suicide squad." Like firemen poised to put out a sudden flame, these men were loaded with liquid cadmium, a solution that absorbs neutrons. If something went wrong with the experiment and it got out of control, these three men would attempt to halt the test.

Fermi stood before the silent crowd of colleagues. Finally, Fermi spoke to explain what was about to happen. His coworker, George Weil, stood by to help with the demonstration. According to Fermi's wife, Laura Fermi, in *Atoms in the Family*, Fermi described the event to the crowd, as follows:

The pile is not performing now because inside it there are rods of cadmium which absorb neutrons. One single rod is sufficient to prevent a chain reaction. So our first step will be to pull out of the pile all control rods. This rod, that we have pulled out with the others, is automatically controlled. Should the intensity of the reaction become greater than a pre-set limit, this rod would go back inside the pile by itself.

This pen will trace a line indicating the intensity of the radiation. When the pile chain-reacts, the pen will trace a line that will go up and up and that will not tend to level off.

In other words, it will be an exponential line. Presently we shall begin our experiment. George will pull out his rod a little at a time. We shall take measurements and verify that the pile will keep on acting as we have calculated.

Weil will first set the rod at thirteen feet [4 m]. This means that thirteen feet of the rod will still be inside the pile. The counters will click faster and the pen will move up to this point and then its trace will level off.

When Enrico Fermi finished explaining to the crowd what was about to happen, he said to Weil, "Go ahead, George."

All eyes were fastened on the pen. It rose and then stopped right where Fermi said it would. It did that time after time all morning until Fermi called for a lunch break. When they returned, the process was started over again. At 3:20 in the afternoon, the pen began to rise and this time it did not level off. A chain reaction had occurred! The experiment was an unqualified success. For twenty-eight minutes, everyone watched as the world's first reactor did just as they had hoped and not as they had feared.

When the experiment was over, Fermi was presented with a bottle of wine. Everyone shared a drink and signed the straw cover of the wine bottle. For everyone there, the truth was evident: the atomic bomb had shifted from an intriguing possibility to a reality. ■

3

FROM A CHAIN REACTION TO A BOMB

As World War II raged on, development of a workable atom bomb continued as well. Recognizing that scientists would need far more room to develop their new weapon, Groves purchased 59,000 acres (23,876 hectares), which was called Site X, in northeastern Tennessee in September 1942. It was the first of several land purchases he would make to see this project through to the end. Approximately 50,000 workers began assembling some of the biggest industrial buildings in the world. In less than two years, there were three production plants producing U-235. By late July 1944, the experts reported that they had enough to make a bomb.

A huge breakthrough came when scientists realized that plutonium could fission like uranium. Producing it was far easier than trying to sort out U-235 from U-238. It was not long before the lab was faced with the previous dilemma of needing more space. Land was purchased in southeast Washington State along the Columbia River. It was a hectic place to be, with 45,000 workers cramped together. They not only had to deal with insect attacks and sandstorms but, in order to maintain security, they also were not told exactly what they were doing beyond their own individual jobs. Morale was low, and fights were common.

Finally, on September 13, 1944, Fermi inserted a fuel slug into the first industrial-sized nuclear reactor. For the next two weeks, this Pile B was loaded and tested. On September 27, the safety rods were taken out. To everyone's relief, fission chain reactions began just as they had hoped. Amazingly, Pile B was a million times more powerful than Pile One had been in Chicago.

THE SECRET SITE OF LOS ALAMOS

Now that the technology was known, it was time for the next phase of the project—building a bomb that could be tested. To prepare for this moment, Robert Oppenheimer (1904–1967), a theoretical physicist from New York City who had been part of the project since 1941, had already scouted out a new location in a remote area in northern New Mexico.

It came as a shock to the students of the Los Alamos Ranch School when they were told that the military needed their school for the war effort. By mid-January 1943, the former school had become Site Y. Unlike the other two sites, the Los Alamos site was a maximum security

Here is an aerial view of the site of the Trinity Test, twenty-four hours after the explosion. The asphalt pavement of the site was turned into a translucent jade. The tower, along with the bomb's wooden platform had been vaporized. As far as 800 yards (731 m) away, wild jackrabbits were killed and the door was blown off of an old farmhouse.

The purchase of Site X, located 20 miles (32 km) west of Knoxville, Tennessee, was Leslie Groves' first official act as brigadier general directing the atom bomb project. A town literally had to be built to accommodate what was first estimated to be 13,000 workers but resulted in 45,000. Here, scientists sorted through uranium to accumulate a sufficient enough amount of the right kind to make an atom bomb. At the time, the town was the fifth-largest city in Tennessee.

Edward Teller was one of the first scientists to become part of the Manhattan Project. At Los Alamos, he headed the theoretical physics division. His strong push for the building of the hydrogen bomb during his time at Los Alamos caused much tension between himself and other scientists there.

military reservation. The 4,000 civilians and 2,000 military personnel it housed were not allowed to let others know where they lived. The entire area was surrounded by barbed wire and the perimeters were under constant patrol by armed soldiers. Its very existence was top secret.

The experts at Los Alamos were divided into four groups: theoretical physics, chemistry, metallurgy (the science and technology of metals), and experimental physics. Their work was exciting but also frightening. At one point, Hungarian-born physicist Edward Teller, who had become a naturalized U.S. citizen in 1941, theorized that the blast from an atom bomb would be so intensely hot that it might ignite the atmosphere itself. Although others hastened to prove him wrong, it was an image that haunted many workers daily. Teller would later become known as the father of the hydrogen bomb that would follow the atom bomb.

One of the questions that the experts grappled with at Los Alamos was just how to control this weapon. They decided to make it

The scientists at Los Alamos had been afraid that if an atomic chain reaction did not occur, it would be a waste of the very rare plutonium that would have been exploded by the TNT used in the bomb. Therefore, "Jumbo" was built—the steel vessel in which the plutonium was stored. When the scientists were confident that the bomb design would work well and they did not need Jumbo, they placed it 800 yards (731 m) from ground zero at the Trinity Test. It survived the explosion intact.

in two pieces so that neither half could explode without the other. When the pieces slammed together, the chain reaction would start. In less than a millionth of a second, the blast would occur. Experts concluded that instead of blowing outward, this bomb needed to implode, the opposite of explode. A ball of plutonium would be surrounded by an explosive that would blow inward toward the plutonium, and the shock waves would compress the plutonium into the size of an eyeball until it exploded.

TRACKING TRAITORS

As careful as the military was being about the security around the atom bomb's design, it was not enough. One of the men working on the idea of implosion was a scientist who had other motives in mind. Instead of working hard to create a bomb that might help the United States win the war, he was harboring secrets that he was about to share. Klaus Fuchs (1911–1988), this German scientist, was considered one of America's most dedicated and talented scientists, yet he would prove to be a traitor. Throughout the winter of 1943 and summer of 1944, he

HITLER ON ATOM BOMB DEVELOPMENT

The fear that physicists under Hitler's Nazi regime would be the first to develop the atom bomb was the driving force behind the efforts of physicists supporting the Allied cause. However, Albert Speer, Hitler's minister of armaments and war productions would later remark that atomic fission and its possibilities were only mentioned once in his many briefings with Hitler. Although Hitler saw its prospects, he didn't think it was possible in his lifetime, and moreover, did not think the chain reaction could be controlled, remarking he did not care to transform Earth into a glowing star under his rule.

Ethel and Julius Rosenberg insisted they were innocent of selling atomic secrets to the Soviet Union up to the time of their execution in 1953. Supporters of the couple at the time felt that the case against them was weak. However, documents released by the Venona project, a joint effort between the United States and the United Kingdom to decode secret messages between the KGB and the Soviet Union, did clearly show they were involved in espionage.

was passing detailed design sketches and handwritten notes to a contact called "Raymond." Raymond was actually an American chemist named Harry Gold who was, in turn, selling these secrets to the Soviet Union. Along with Fuchs's information, Raymond was also receiving sketches from a machinist at Los Alamos named David Greenglass.

All the workers at Los Alamos were watched very closely, yet these two men managed to pass information along without being caught for a long time. It was not until 1949 that the Federal Bureau of Investigation (FBI) confronted Fuchs with accusations of being a spy. He eventually confessed and on March 1, 1950, the jury deliberated for only two hours before finding him guilty of communicating information to the Soviets. He was sentenced to fourteen years in prison and served nine of them before being released and returning to East Germany. Gold was also caught by the FBI. He spent sixteen years in prison.

Greenglass's story was slightly different. When he was arrested, he accused his sister, Ethel Rosenberg, and her husband, Julius, of being spies. He agreed to testify against them in exchange for not being executed. According to Greenglass, he took information from Los Alamos and gave it to the couple. Ethel typed it up and gave it to Russia's KGB. Although the Rosenbergs claimed innocence, they were convicted of treason in 1951. They were executed in New York's Sing Sing prison on June 19, 1953, the first American civilians in history to be executed for espionage, or spying. In 2001, Greenglass admitted that he lied about his sister's involvement.

THE DAY FINALLY ARRIVES

On April 12, 1945, President Roosevelt died and his vice president, Harry Truman, was sworn in as leader of the nation. Less than a month later, Germany surrendered and suddenly the war in Europe was over. Everyone could relax a little now that the threat of Germany creating a bomb first was no longer a concern. All was not calm, though, because the war was still going strong in the Pacific. American bombers were attacking Japanese cities daily, and Truman was involved in talks with

In which I tell Stalin
we expect to drop the most
powerful explosive had made on
the Japanese. He smiled and said
he appreciated my telling him
but he did not know what I was

Joseph Stalin, Harry Truman, and Winston Churchill are pictured *(top, left to right)* at the Potsdam Conference that lasted from July to August 1945. The Big Three had met to discuss postwar arrangements for Europe and declare an ultimatum to the Japanese. Meanwhile, pressure was on at Los Alamos to successfully test the atom bomb. Truman wrote this note *(bottom)*, describing how he told Stalin about the bomb. Stalin was reported to have shown no special interest. It is believed he knew of the Trinity Test from his agents within the United States.

The Trinity Test was not intended to be a full-scale atom bomb test. The scientists at Los Alamos were confident in one part of the bomb's design: the uranium trigger gun. They only needed to evaluate the implosion weapon design. The Gadget, pictured here, was the name given to this implosion device. The outer casing, covered with cables and detonators, held the plutonium core that was the size of an orange and weighed 13.5 pounds (6.1 kg).

Joseph Stalin to see if he could count on the Soviet Union's help to continue the fight. Before he left the United States for the Potsdam Conference that took place in Berlin in July 1945 between himself, Stalin, and Winston Churchill, the British prime minister, he was brought up-to-date about the progress of the atom bomb. If it worked as everyone hoped, he would use it as his ace in the hole to sway the Soviets to America's side in the upcoming meeting.

Oppenheimer shared the news that it was time to test the atom bomb with scientists back at the University of California, Berkeley, who had helped create the bomb's design. In a cryptic, coded telegram he stated: "Any time after the 15th would be a good time for our fishing trip, because we are not certain of the weather we may be delayed several days." Bets were taken on the size of the blast, with

Often referred to as the father of the atomic bomb, Robert Oppenheimer went on to become the chairman of the General Advisory Committee to the Atomic Energy Commission. He strongly opposed the building of the hydrogen bomb, pitting him against Edward Teller. When Oppenheimer was accused of Communist sympathies, Teller testified against him, causing Oppenheimer to lose his security clearance by the government.

everyone throwing in one dollar. Guesses ranged from zero to 45,000 tons; the winning bet was 18,000 and the prize was $102.

The site where the test bomb would be detonated was approximately 200 miles (322 km) south of Los Alamos. It was a rather desolate stretch called Jornada del Muerto, or "Journey of the Dead." The area was 24 miles by 17 miles (39 km by 28 km) and in the middle was a 100-foot (30.5 m) tower with a shed at the top that housed the bomb.

The test had been nicknamed Trinity and was initially set for 4:00 AM on July 16, but due to a thunderstorm, it was postponed until 5:30 AM. It was a long and tedious wait for everyone involved. Finally, the moment arrived. Flares lit the sky, and sirens blared a warning. The firing team climbed up to the tower, set all the switches, and six quickly took shelter in a concrete bunker 6 miles (10 km) away. The base station was 10 miles (16 km) away, and many of the scientists and other interested parties gathered there to experience the history-making event.

> "By twenty or thirty seconds after the explosion I was regaining normal vision."
>
> *Robert Serber*

At 5:29:45 AM, the world's first atom bomb went off. The tower it was sitting on was vaporized, and the sand around it melted into a glassy, green, fused desert sand. The explosion created a saucer-shaped crater a quarter-mile across. It was considered a complete success.

EYEWITNESSES TO TRINITY'S POWER

Eyewitness accounts of the Trinity Test were included in the Manhattan Engineer District Records national archives in Washington, D.C. Here are a few extracts from their experiences that day.

Enrico Fermi's perspective on the blast was the technical one expected from a scientist so closely involved with the project. At the time, Fermi was stationed at the base camp about 10 miles (16 km) from the site of the explosion.

I had my face protected by a large board in which a piece of dark welding glass had been inserted. My first impression of the explosion was the very intense flash of light and a sensation of heat on the parts of my body that were exposed. Although I did not look directly towards the object, I had the impression that suddenly the countryside became brighter than in full daylight . . . About 40 seconds after the explosion, the air blast reached me. I tried to estimate its strength by dropping from about six feet [1.8 m] small pieces of paper before, during and after the passage of the blast wave. Since, at the time, there was no wind I could observe very distinctly and actually measure the displacement of the pieces of paper that were in the process of falling while the blast was passing. The shift was about 2 meters [6.6 feet], which, at the time, I estimated to correspond to the blast that would be produced by 10,000 tons of T.N.T.

Another eyewitness, Dr. Luis W. Alvarez, was one of the team members at Los Alamos. He had a front-row seat to the event, because he was riding in a B-29 only 20 miles (32 km) from the site. He wrote:

My first sensation was one of intense light covering my whole field of vision. This seemed to last for about 1/2 second after which I noted an intense orange-red glow through the clouds . . . In about eight minutes the top of the cloud was at approximately 40,000 feet [12,192 m] as close as I could estimate from our altitude of 24,000 feet [7,315 m] . . . I did not feel the shock wave hit the plane but the pilot felt the reaction on the rudder through the rudder pedals.

Robert Serber, leader of the theoretical physics group at Los Alamos, described the event from a bunker 20 miles (32 km) away:

At the instant of the explosion, I was looking directly at it, with no eye protection of any kind. I saw first a yellow glow, which grew instantly into an overwhelmingly white flash, so intense that I was completely blinded . . . By twenty or thirty seconds after the explosion I was regaining normal vision . . . Some time later, the noise of the explosion reached us. It had

Witnesses to the Trinity Test explosion first saw the front of the shock wave, then a huge fireball. The smoke didn't rise into a mushroom cloud until two seconds after the blast. This photograph captures the explosion at least seven seconds after detonation.

the quality of distant thunder, but was louder. The sound, due to reflections from nearby hills, returned and repeated and reverberated for several seconds, very much like thunder . . . The grandeur and magnitude of the phenomenon were completely breathtaking.

Kenneth Greisen was in the group of men who had prepared and installed the bomb's detonators. He wrote that tension was high as his team waited for the blast.

If the shot turned out to be a dud, it might possibly be our fault. We were pretty sure we had done our job well, but there is always some chance of a slip . . . The heat and light were as though the sun had just come out with unusual brilliance . . . A tremendous cloud of smoke was pouring upwards, some parts having brilliant red and yellow colors, like clouds at sunset . . . At this time I believe I exclaimed, "My god, it worked!" and felt a great relief . . . Between the appearance of light and the arrival of the sound, there was loud cheering in the group around us. After the noise was over, we all went about congratulating each other and shaking hands. I believe we were all much more shaken up by the shot mentally than physically.

Oppenheimer later described how people laughed, cried, or were silent, and how he knew from that moment on that the world would never be the same. On the other hand, Groves would depict it as successful beyond anyone's imagination.

AN ELATED PRESIDENT

When President Truman received news that the test was successful, he was elated. He knew that with a weapon of that caliber, he did not need the Soviet Union's assistance to overcome the Japanese. On July 26, at the Potsdam Conference in Berlin, the United States, Great Britain, and China sent the Potsdam Declaration to Japan. It stated that Japan must surrender or face "prompt and utter destruction."

For Japan, complete surrender was simply not an option. The Japanese were afraid that their emperor, Hirohito, would be executed, which was unacceptable because he was considered to be a divine, or holy, figure. Two days after they received the Potsdam Declaration, the Japanese responded over their regular radio broadcast. They called the terms of surrender "unworthy of consideration," "absurd," and "presumptuous." The next, most violent phase of the war was directly ahead: President Truman ordered the dropping of the nation's most powerful weapon. ■

> "I believe we were all much more shaken up by the shot mentally than physically."
>
> *Kenneth Greison*

THE POWER
AND PAIN
OF *PIKA–DON*

The president's order had been given, and now it was time for all the years of trial and error to come together into a weapon like the world had never seen before.

The atomic bombs "Little Boy" and "Fat Man" were taken apart and flown to Tinian, a small island in the Pacific Ocean. There, they were reassembled and loaded onto Boeing B-29 bomber planes. Five cities had been selected to be attacked: Kyoto, Hiroshima, Yokohama, Niigata, and Kokura. At the last minute, Nagasaki was added to the list. Besides meeting visual requirements needed for dropping the bomb, Nagasaki was added because it was one of the last major cities in Japan not yet burned out from previous U.S. attacks.

THE ATTACKS

On the morning of August 6, 1945, three B-29 Superfortresses took off from Tinian and headed toward Hiroshima. Loaded in the plane named *Enola Gay* was Little Boy, a 10.5-foot-long (3.2 m) bomb that weighed 9,700 pounds (4,400 kg). Lieutenant Colonel Paul W. Tibbets piloted the plane. He was accompanied by the aircraft *Great Artiste* and *Necessary Evil*. Both were loaded with equipment for photographing and recording the entire event.

At 8:15 AM, Little Boy was dropped over Hiroshima. The bomb exploded 1,900 feet (579 m) above ground level. The city was devastated; buildings were vaporized, asphalt boiled, roofs melted, and telephone poles burst into flames. More than half of Hiroshima's entire population was either killed or injured immediately. As copilot Robert Lewis watched the blast, he is reported to have said to himself, "My God, what have we done?"

It took hours for the populations of other cities of Japan to find out what had happened to Hiroshima. Tokyo residents did not even know that a bomb had been dropped there until they heard it on the White House announcement from Washington sixteen hours later. The event came to be called *pika-don* by the survivors. It meant "flash-bang," symbolizing the sight and sound of the terrifying explosion.

Despite the incredible destruction, Japan refused to surrender. Believing that the United States only had one atomic bomb, the Japanese did not waiver. President Truman decided that a second bomb

This is a photo of the remains of Nagasaki Medical College after the atom bomb Fat Man was dropped over Nagasaki. The bomb was strategically dropped over an area of the city to do the maximum damage to industry.

The flight crews of the B-29 bombers that would drop the atomic bombs study plans and aerial photographs of their targets. Inset: Paul W. Tibbets Jr., the pilot of *Enola Gay*, named the bomber after his mother, who had once assured the pilot he would never be killed flying. Here, he waves from his cockpit before takeoff.

STAGGERING STATISTICS

ESTIMATES OF THE NUMBERS OF CASUALTIES

	Pre raid population	Dead	Injured	Total Casualties
Hiroshima	225,000	66,000	69,000	135,000
Nagasaki	195,000	39,000	25,000	64,000

(http://www.yale.edu/lawweb/avalon/abomb/mp10.htm)

ESTIMATES OF THE CAUSES OF CASUALTIES

	Burns	Falling Debris	Flying Glass	Other
Hiroshima	60%	30%	NA	10%
Nagasaki	95%	9%	7%	7%

(http://www.yale.edu/lawweb/avalon/abomb/mp10.htm)

had to be dropped immediately if Japan was to be convinced, so he ordered the next attack. Although this bomb was headed to Kokura, heavy cloud coverage diverted pilot Major Charles W. Sweeney. Instead, the Fat Man bomb was dropped on Nagasaki. This bomb exploded 1,600 feet (488 m) above ground level. Although the casualties were less in this city, they were still absolutely overwhelming. People were killed by the blast of heat, as well as from the debris of collapsing buildings and shards of flying glass.

Although there was a third atomic bomb ready, President Truman decided against using it. At this point, he was uncomfortable with the

The Little Boy atom bomb was 10.5 feet (3.2 m) long with a diameter of 29 inches (74 cm), and weighed 9,700 pounds (4,400 kg). Little Boy was the first and last bomb of its kind to use uranium as the source of explosive energy (Fat Man used plutonium, as did Gadget in the Trinity Test). Little Boy was considered easy to detonate. It used a standard gun-type trigger. The chance of this trigger mechanism failing was calculated at one in 10,000.

huge numbers of people who had been killed in the first two attacks, so he decided not to sign the order for another one.

Even after the two attacks, Japan's leaders were still ambivalent about surrender. Finally, they called upon Emperor Hirohito and asked him what they should do. He could not bear to see the people of his country struggle any longer. He felt that ending the war was the only way to bring world peace and lift the burden of horrible distress that had now occurred.

After some negotiation, Japan accepted the terms of the surrender. Emperor Hirohito made a formal statement over the radio on August 14, 1945. It was the first time the people of Japan had heard the voice of their leader:

> Despite the best that has been done by everyone . . . the war situation has developed not necessarily to Japan's advantage, while the general trends of the world have all turned against her interests. Moreover, the enemy has begun to employ a new and most cruel bomb, the power of which to do damage is indeed incalculable, taking the toll of many innocent lives . . . This is the reason why We have ordered the acceptance of the provisions of the Joint declaration of the Powers . . . The hardships and sufferings to which Our nation is to be subjected hereafter will be certainly great. We are keenly aware of the inmost [sic] feelings of all ye, Our subjects. However it is according to the dictate of time and fate that We have resolved to pave the way for a grand peace for all generations to come by enduring the unendurable and suffering what is insufferable.

VICTORY AND REMORSE

Although the United States was the victor in this battle, it was not without a good measure of regret. Many scientists were filled with feelings of guilt. Some quit the field entirely, while others refused to ever work on a piece of weaponry again. Even Dr. Edward Teller was quoted as saying,

Mushroom clouds billowed over Hiroshima after Little Boy was dropped. After leaving the plane, the bomb nosed down and exploded forty-three seconds later. After the bomb's release, *Enola Gay* suddenly jumped because it was four tons lighter. Robert Lewis, the copilot of the mission, said that he would never get over the memory of dropping the bomb on this city.

"To develop the bomb was right. To drop it was wrong." Before either of the bombs were dropped, Szilard, along with more than sixty other scientists from the Met Lab, signed a petition to President Truman, voicing their doubts about using the bomb against Japan. With the war in Europe over, they were not certain bombing Japan was the right solution. The petition asked Truman to warn Japan that the United States had a massively powerful bomb that it would use if Japan continued to refuse to surrender. They also asked the president to consider the moral responsibilities of using a weapon like the atom bomb. They feared, as did many others, that to do so would only allow more and more destruction in the future. Szilard wrote:

> The development of atomic power will provide the nations with new means of destruction. The atomic

The Memorial Cenotaph at Peace Park in the heart of Hiroshima is dedicated to Japan's victims of the atom bomb. The chest below the arch holds the death registry of the victims of the bomb. The arch resembles an ancient arch-shaped house and symbolically provides shelter for the victims' souls. Hiroshima, today, is known as an international city of peace and culture.

bombs at our disposal represent only the first step in this direction, and there is almost no limit to the destructive power which will become available in the course of future development. Thus, a nation which set the precedent of using these newly liberated forces of nature for purposes of destruction may have to bear the responsibility of opening the door to an era of devastation on an unimaginable scale.

As passionate as this petition was, it was never seen by President Truman. Groves had chosen not to pass it on to the president.

The statistics from the actual explosions were horrifying, and they only continued to climb as the effects of radiation illness began to appear in those who survived the original events. Sometimes these effects took only days to appear; other times it was months. Diseases such as leukemia and cancer killed thousands more long after the smoke had cleared and the fires were out. In general, people had not

A stopped watch forever memorializes 8:15 AM, the time on August 6, 1945, that the atom bomb was dropped on Hiroshima. The night before the bombing, the city's residents spent a fearful night listening to the sounds of sirens as warnings of air raids were drilled, but by that morning, the sirens ended and people were busy with their morning routines.

been warned of the existence or the threat of radiation poisoning that accompanied the bomb.

The decision to drop the atom bomb on Japan had not been an easy one for the United States, and numerous arguments exist for its use. Was it possible that Japan would have surrendered without the use of the atom bomb? Judging by the resistance the United States had faced in the Pacific theater of World War II, some experts believed this was unlikely. There

> "To develop the bomb was right. To drop it was wrong."
>
> *Dr. Edward Teller*

had already been enormous casualties on both sides. If the war had continued, perhaps that number would have surpassed the casualties caused by the dropping of the bombs. There is also the argument that the dropping of the bombs was a threat to the Soviet Union, the Communist superpower that was now the chief rival of the United States following the war. Moreover, a quick surrender by the Japanese, without the United States asking the Soviet Union for assistance in the effort, meant the Soviet Union would not be involved in the postwar occupation of Japan—as was happening throughout Europe after the defeat of the Axis powers in the European theater of the war.

Although many Americans were relieved to see the war end at last, they were equally horror-struck at the lives lost and the destruction in Japan. In 1958, a monument was erected in Hiroshima to honor all those who had died. Engraved on the memorial are the words, "Repose ye in peace, for the error shall never be repeated." It was a fragile promise since the United States has already moved on to testing even more powerful bombs. The end was not in sight; the world of weapons of mass destruction had only just begun. ■

[GLOSSARY]

alchemist A person who practices the art of alchemy, a medieval philosophy that aimed to change base metals into gold.

atom The smallest particle of an element that still maintains the element's properties.

divine Holy.

electron A subatomic particle with a negative electric charge.

fission The process of splitting into parts.

fluoresce To emit electromagnetic radiation.

graphite A soft, steel-gray type of carbon with a metallic luster and greasy feel.

implode To collapse violently inward.

KGB The Soviet Union's security and intelligence organization.

leukemia A disease affecting the bone marrow and white blood cell production.

neutrons A subatomic particle with a neutral charge.

nucleus The core or central portion of an atom.

pacifist A person opposed to settling conflict with violence.

pika-don Japanese name for the atom bombs dropped on Hiroshima and Nagasaki.

pitchblende A mineral ore containing uranium and radium.

protons A subatomic particle with a positive electric charge.

tedious Tiresome due to length or dullness.

thermal Using, producing, or made of heat.

treason The betrayal of one's country.

[FOR MORE] INFORMATION

The Avalon Project at Yale Law School
127 Wall Street
New Haven, CT 06520
Web site: http://www.yale.edu/lawweb/avalon/avalon.htm

Nuclear Age Peace Foundation
PMB 121
1187 Coast Village Road, Suite 1
Santa Barbara, CA 93108-2794
(805) 965-3443
e-mail: wagingpeace@napf.org

"Race for the Superbomb"
PBS Productions
Web site: http://www.pbs.org/wgbh/amex/bomb/index.html

WEB SITES
Due to the changing nature of Internet links, the Rosen Publishing Group, Inc., has developed an online list of Web sites related to the subject of this book. This site is updated regularly. Please use this link to access the list:

http://www.rosenlinks.com/lwmd/atbo/

[FOR FURTHER]
READING

Anderson, Dale. *The Atom Bomb Project*. Milwaukee: World Almanac, 2004.

Cooper, Dan. *Enrico Fermi: And the Revolutions of Modern Physics*. New York: Oxford University Press, 1999.

Gallant, Roy A. *The Ever-Changing Atom*. Tarrytown, NY: Benchmark Books, 2000.

Lace, William W. *The Atom Bomb*. San Diego: Lucent Books, 2001.

Scheibach, Michael. *Atomic Narratives and American Youth: Coming of Age with the Atom, 1945–1955*. Jefferson, NC: McFarland and Company, 2003.

Seddon, Tom. *Atom Bomb*. New York: W. H. Freeman and Company, 1995.

Sherrow, Victoria. *The Making of the Atom Bomb*. San Diego: Lucent Books, 2000.

[BIBLIOGRAPHY]

Gallant, Roy A. *The Ever-Changing Atom*. Tarrytown, NY: Benchmark Books, 2000.

Rhodes, Richard. *The Making of the Atomic Bomb*. New York: Simon & Schuster, 1986.

Seddon, Tom. *Atom Bomb*. New York: W. H. Freeman and Company, 1995.

Winkler, Allan M. *The Cold War: A History in Documents*. New York: Oxford University Press, 2000.

[INDEX]

ABOUT THE AUTHOR

Tamra Orr is the author of more than three dozen nonfiction books for children and young adults. She has a bachelor of science degree in education from Ball State University and recently moved across the country from Indiana to Portland, Oregon. She lives between the mountains and the ocean and is the homeschooling mother of four children, ages eight to twenty, as well as a wife to Joseph.

PHOTO CREDITS

Cover, pp. 7, 33, 42–43, 49 (right), 51 © Still Picture Branch, National Archives and Records Administration; pp. 4–5 © Rene Burri/Magnum Photos; p. 6 © Scott Camazine/Photo Researchers, Inc.; pp. 9, 10–11, 12, 14, 20–21, 22 © Hulton/Archive/Getty Images; p. 16 © Time Life Pictures/Getty Images; p. 19 Franklin D. Roosevelt Presidential Library/National Archives and Records Administration; pp. 25, 28, 37 (bottom), 38, 48–49 © Corbis; pp. 30–31, 37 (top), 53 © Bettmann/Corbis; p. 32 © Wayne Miller/Magnum Photos; p. 35 © AP/Wide World Photos; p. 39 © Philippe Halsman/Magnum Photos; p. 46 © Underwood & Underwood/Corbis; p. 54–55 © David Samuel Robbins/Corbis; p. 56 © Topham/The Image Works.

Design: Evelyn Horovicz; Editor: Leigh Ann Cobb; Layout: Thomas Forget; Photo Researcher: Fernanda Rocha